MW00527030

Dwell

Written and Illustrated by

Nashé

To Mami, Daddy, Grammie, Pop, Betty, Natalie,
Kahlia, Angel, Mari, Asia, Destiny, Kiara, Sarah,
Teraria, Sasha, Angelina, Stacey, Nadine, Janelle,
Bre, Briah, Asiah, Taylor, Savannah, David, Mandi,
Zaria, Teddy, Mickey, Stephens, Amanda, JG, Siaara,
Brittany, Jalisha, Tammy, Susan, Che'Le, Ashley,
BriAnna, Tricia, Israel, Trés, Kate, Sydney, Alexis,
Meliah, Lia, Ericka, Ayne, DiMaur, Curtis, Drew

For my closest friends. Having been treasured books
on my bookshelf. Always there when I reach
for you in times of need. A tether to this world
when I begin to feel lost and out of place. Your words
more scripture and necessity than you realize. Pray
you know the value in your dog eared pages
and worn use from cover to cover.
I love you. Thank you.

This is my journey

When you left you took a piece of me with you
Mommy's scared I'll look for it in boys that are no good for me
I'm scared that all I'll see is you leaving whenever a boy looks at me
I cried for you
So why didn't you hear my pleas with the same ear you pressed to my
mom's pregnant belly
Why weren't you there
Why wasn't I good enough
Was it my fault
I must not have been good enough
These were the things etched into my mind
Left there by your leaving
This must have been something like magic
The disappearing act of a true magician
These spells were something like deceiving
But this wizardry lasted longer than any show time
This magic is forever stuck in my memory
Forever playing over and over again like a broken record
So I went looking for a different kind of magic
In the back of the car on a star filled night
I whispered wishes into the wind
Sending prayers to anyone who was listening
You would come back soon
My wishes wouldn't be wasted
I wouldn't be just another teary eyed kid wishing on stars
But years past
And those wishes kept going unanswered
Pieces of me were missing

Things about me were unexplained
You made up pieces and parts of me
I couldn't figure them out for anything
I wonder if you were thinking of me the way I was always thought of you
Always dreamed of you
Always wished for a father's strong embrace
And always hoping to see your love for me etched onto your face
Why wasn't I good enough
Why did I make you want to leave
Dang if I didn't feel like you were clipping wings
Putting them in your pocket as you walked out the door
And so I never learned to fly
And it was hard for me to sing
Because singing meant joy
And it seemed like you packed that too with all the things you took with you
Why did you take so many things with you
I don't even know if you wanted to leave
But I didn't know what else to believe
And even so I hoped that everyday you regretted it
I hoped you felt the same ache in your chest that I felt in mine
Then at least I would know one thing we shared
Because we never shared moments
Not moments that I could remember
No memories for me to hold on to
I despised the fact that anything we had together was a faded memory
Something lost to me a long time ago
I hated story books for the way they portrayed father's
Because you weren't ever there to tuck me in at night
And you never kissed my forehead and told me I was the most beautiful girl in the world
My plotline carried potholes
My story line wasn't picture perfect
And in my storyline as the main character I didn't even know if it was worth it
If I was worth it

It's so crazy how you could miss someone you never even truly knew
There were so many things I didn't understand about you
So many things I wanted to ask
I always missed you more than minutes ticked into hours
And I kept wishing on those stars
Those glittering beams of hope that were laced with the things dreams
were made of
I found out earlier than most little girls that fairytales weren't real
So when little girls were wishing for their prince charming I was
wishing for my daddy back
When other little girls dreamed of the prince saving them from dragons
I wished you would come and save me from all my doubts
Somehow I always knew I wasn't good enough
And the day I found out that stars were only balls of gas millions miles
away I cried
For all my wasted wishing and all these false hopes
My cries were laced with broken dreams
Because stars weren't laced with the things dreams are made of
And it didn't seem like you were ever coming back
And yet on star filled nights in the back of the car I still found myself
wishing on stars

Wishing On Stars

I lost God in a whole bunch of me
And you pulled me up by the tips of my fingers
I almost risked losing me and you and God too
In a whole bunch of drowning
When did it get so hard to breath
So easy to get lost

Safety

Sometimes it isn't about having the money to fix it
At times it's about the time people are willing to take out
The energy people are willing to allow you to take up
"Not right now Nashé, I'm on the phone."
"Not right now Nashé, I'm driving."
"Not right now Nashé, I'm busy."
"Not right now Nashé, my life is still going on."
I was called a liar more times than I have fingers and toes to count
When I was talking about my illness
I knew I was sick long before anybody was willing to believe me
I wasn't unloved
But maybe seen as a little overdramatic
It's been years since I told my mom
How I wanted to slice open my insides if only to see my own darkness
spill out
Two years since I told her how angry I was at this body
And I am still here
I asked four times to be evaluated
It took two doctors to confirm that something was wrong
And there are still a lot of days when there are doubts
Wants to wish away my illness
No one wants me to not be the easy child anymore
My brother was two handfuls on his own
No one had anything else to try and grasp my problems with
My mom didn't have any hands left for me
And I never blamed anyone
I only prayed for her
And me too sometimes because I'm so lucky to be here
I'm so lucky to be able to be here with you today
Because I had way too many days where I didn't know if I would make
it
Because I have seen far too many people prove how easy it is to die
I'm so glad I chose to live
I've had people chop my disease into little pieces
Insignificant and less of an issue
Just to make it easier for them to swallow
Make me feel silly for the whale that I made this little minnow out to be

But I know my illness's shark teeth all too well
Felt those sharp teeth more times than coins in wishing wells
Some people may never understand

Convenience

You are so beautiful
That is what they chose to sustain you
Those words that you lived on
The only thing they spoon fed you
It is amazing
Fresh spring water on a hot day
Until that is the only thing you live for
You never realized those were words that starved you
Forever scarred you
Left you incomplete
Broken
A shell of the woman you were destined to be
And it made you monstrous
Withheld any true meaning you would have
Sickly sweet
A trap of would have beens and could have beens
The taste in your mouth always seems more bitter sweet
Lifelessness left just under the surface
No one really sees
They weren't ever looking for it anyway
Maybe you didn't seem broken anyway

Lack Of

When I was born I was already a little less soft than expected
A little more tender than anticipated
I had been fighting for my mom's attention since I was young
Too much going on and not enough eyes to go around
I lost tender ages to life lessons
Me and my mother were soul sisters
Bound together in a different way
A little less soul and a little more concrete
A real life blood bond between her and me
And that's what she gave me
Real life in the palm of her hand
And I respected her for that
But that didn't mean I would be her way
Her life lessons struck my heart in such a way
Pushed me further to something she wasn't
Less riotous blood
More peace
A little more soft
Weak
Nashé you have to stop crying about everything
I was never the mountainous empire she thought she built of me
Never the war she expected of me
A softness of moonlight
That she didn't know she would see

Mothers make us war

We pin shadows to our shoulders
Trying to stand them up on their own
Instead of dragging these weights
By the heels of our feet
Maybe them standing on their own two feet
Will make them less of a burden
More foe to defeat
Than our own inhibitions

More Threat

I'm something like part day dream part broken fantasy
Part I want to love you more
But you were never even a friend to me
The wreckage of fragmented moments heave in my chest
With each breath
I wonder where you'll be on my last
Probably in the air somewhere
Making it known that you are not to be forgotten
These memories have made crystal glass of my heart
Fragile but beautiful
It glistens and shines in the sun like a star in the night sky

Wreckage

In the world in which I bring my son into there are things I must teach him
At dinner I'll pass him survival tips like mom please pass me the salt
Giving him strategy as if I was sending him off to war
I will be sending him off to a world at war
A world that didn't deem him worthy
And though I would treat him as a king
The world would deem him as peasant
Lower than them
Unworthy of justice
He'll find that gun barrels are always shorter than alleyways
And gun barrels always lead to shorter endings than alleyways
In the world in which I bring my son into there are things I must teach him
Keep your head down
keep your voice low
Don't draw too much attention to yourself
I don't want to see your outline drawn on a sidewalk
Please be respectful
Avoid any confusion with the police
Pull your pants up
Keep your hands out of your pockets
It is better to be silent than to be silenced
Oh please dear son of mine understand that I didn't want you to come into a world of war
But all because of your skin it seems you're going to fighting a losing war
I don't want to see you shot down
I just want to lift you up
But they'll shoot you even with your hands up
 And I don't want it to be about race
But people can never tell me it's not about race
The race between running feet and a bullet with my future son's name carved on it
I never want to have to see a grave with his name carved on it
I won't ever be ready to bury a child
Not anyone's
Let alone my own
I've know his name since the third grade
But more and more lately it seems his name will be mine to know alone
Because I'm scared of the world of war he would meet
The world would knock him down

I will always want to help him up
But they won't want to see him on his feet
He'll only be a hero if he dribbles a ball or messes with mics
There will always be people trying to change his fate
People keep falling and there are many more
And to those who have fallen I'm afraid my son will be able to relate
I need you to understand
They turn boys who look like you
From little boys to latest hashtags within seconds
So future son I hope you will listen to these things and learn them well
Because in the world in which I bring you into there are many things I
must teach you

Things I Must Teach my Son

I don't ever want to see a grave with his name carved on it

12/10/14 - ∞

I'm often left to wonder if people are as human as I am
I wonder if empathy is foreign to them
I ponder the things that might fill their hearts content
Do they cry the same salt water tears
Are they scared when faced with their deepest fears
Do their demons try to tear them down at their weakest
Do they have weakness
Will I find sureness where doubt is supposed to lie
Do they feel any guilt in telling a lie
Can they find truth in stories of heartbreak
I wonder if in their hearts I could find sympathy
If in their hearts there might be treachery
Can they feel that nervousness of anxiety
I wonder if they think about finding a place society
If life gets hard and things slip away from them do they feel empty
Or can they not help feeling nothing
Do their hearts ache to feel something
What do they do if they can't feel anything
Are they ever faced with their mortality
Can they ever get scared of ending up like the majority
Do they get scared of things that are new
Would they look forward to the future if they only knew
I'm always left to wonder if people feel as human as I do

Humanity

When unease is no longer fed
She growls loudly
She is no longer this small gnawing thing
But of demand and determination
She is angry
She orders you answer her
How dare you leave her dying here
You need her
Afterall
She is the only one that has been
There for you all this time
When no one else was

Anxiety

In which I no longer check for bruises
I've known my scars
Long since had introductions and knew
Each of their names with such confidence
I am prepared for healing
In the same way that a plant blooming in the desert is desperate
For rain
Not to be rid of my scars
But only to know them better
Understand what they need
So that this body can survive
As many droughts as possible

Desert Flower

Hey
Pay attention
Are you listening
Keep your head out of the clouds
How many times do I have to tell you
For God sake
Are
      You
            Listening

My first name

For my grandmother Debra
Who picked each letter with the utmost care
Fresh sunflowers from a garden
Ever undeserving of such meticulous work
Such thought-full preparing
A mass of prayers in each syllable
I'm sorry for complaining about the way it is spelled
Those that mispronounce it
Just didn't capture the essence my grandmother could
Her dwelling in my first name
Is what creates the calm in my smile
Right before the storm

      My middle name

For my mother
Ever a rebel with the biggest cause
A stronger heart behind every one
To live fearlessly with abandon
And without regret
Every calendar year
Another mark of some amazing achievement
Enough drive to get you across the world and water
And enough tactful mother's intuition to bring you home at night

      My last name

For my father
A name I want etched across my wrist
His youngest daughter
Only child to carry his name

A sole legacy
I wear it around my neck

For name's sake

I've been sitting out
Around four to half past six in the morning
Waiting for the stars to come home
They're tired
Having been up all night
All of the nights
And they are ready to retire
To settle into my belly
To be nurtured by my soul
They want to be warm and close
And rest for a while
Until it is night again

Starry Cove

I asked you if I looked pretty
a daughter asking
Reassurance of her father
A confirmation that you once fell in love with my mother
An affirmation that I could be the image of something you
Loved so once
That you
My maker
Find approval in who I have become
"How do I look, dad?"
I just want to know that you think me worthy
Think me something to be cherished
And looked upon
Something deserving of sacrifice
Love me
Hold me graciously
Careful not to dent this paper thin heart
I have been looking for you
In all the places you are not
I've wanted to know if
You hold distaste for all these pieces
Of you and her
That lay here in my belly tied by this thin string
Of me
Your love not lamb slaughtered on the altar
but more making scarce supplies
Last longer than they should
I begin with apologies
For all that I am not
And all that I am
Pray you not find this
Offering at your feet offensive
I only wish to appease you
To please the un-please-able
I know this offering is scarce
The crops have frozen over
And I have little to give

Wish this sacrifice is to your liking
I could have never prayed a love that big
To know hope and happiness in the same crisp fall breath
The chill wraps around my bones
I can never find shelter in how you feel about me
For walls that could collapse at any moment aren't a home
I seek you out in all the places you are not
"Does this look okay?"

Ressurance

So often roses are born into this world
That only wants to dethrone them
Because they only desire their beauty
If it doesn't come with
Their pain

Pick and Chose

In which my heart and hands are synonymous
I have
Offered my hands to you in your times of need
Easy as breathing to do such things
I do this as second nature
I have stabilized my entire world with my hands
Kept it in my grasp
Just to make sure it is close
I find peace in knowing my hands have had a part in
These taped together pieces of a child's craft
My hands of pure intentions
Of warmth and truth
My hands are long sighs
Of summer afternoons
When the air is sweet
And a pause in conversation feels right

Hands At Work

I've probably met 4 soul mates before the age of 18
People who were meant to pull at my soul with their hearts arms and
fingers
But I met them too early
I met them when we weren't meant to be
So I drop things if I see signs of them wanting to leave
Because they aren't meant for me

Pull At

Every weekend
For the past 12 years of my life
Cleaning has been the top priority
you ain't going nowhere till them chores are done
I wake up every Saturday
To a symphony of Gospel or R&b
Being a procrastinator on chore day
was a cardinal sin in my mother's house
You would get it done
And you would get it done the right way
Her way

Her Clean

The low hum of my fan lulls me to sleep
In the familiar darkness of my room
A dusk that once pulled fears like lost treasures from
An ever abandoned sea
Navy waters that mirror a blank night sky
This darkness that now offers sanction
The same way sanction offers sanity
The way sanity offers peace
Silence in this cumbersome world
Cocoon of warmth
And wouldn't I
Be a treasure to wake up to
Bare back and peaceful
Without a crumbling world in my wake
Serene
But then I remind myself
I don't need to be that for someone else
I wake up to myself every morning
A treasure
A black girl in such a world
That doesn't want us
Though
Black girls are endlessly versatile
Such a shame
That the globe is just getting to
Offer range
How things lead unto things
And as we demand to become more inclusive
I think of a grandmother I never got to meet
A beautiful black woman
Of all trades
A woman who captivated my father
Still to this day
He holds her in his back pocket
Most of the time like a weight he can't get rid of
But I know
Sometimes she echoes in my laughter

And it helps his heart

Back pocket dreams

What of your friends
Of your true companions
Of those you trust and value
Are they safety net enough for this fall
Have they considered and accepted
All your flaws
Have you told the wind of this bond

Support System

Why has every man I have ever known
Been built from tragedy
First something destroys them
And then they destroy everything around them
Is this pain condemning
All consuming
Or just a necessary evil of our male counterparts
I've known their sobered hearts
And drunken minds
Call it chance
Or unlucky happenings
But don't call it fate
And don't name it destiny
These lost boys turn to lost men
How they Peter Pan away their problems
Wish to dream all day
And never grow old
Stuck in some kind of never ever land
Ships on never ending seas
Waves looking more and more like life lines
No longer recognizing the oceans that holds them captive as prison
They make me seasick
How wishing to help them
Feels more and more like jumping
Into a ocean with no idea how to swim
And no life jacket to keep me afloat
Make myself an offering
To the crocodile
With the ticking clock in his belly
They make me feel more like the time bomb
Tonight I pray for them
Wipe their salt water tears away from me
Before I enter prayer
Afraid my God may find their hurt in my heart
Instead of out there (their) in them
I've considered taking up rebuilding men
As a service to myself or them

Am I enough
Do I provide the right construction materials
The right map to get us to the second star to the right
And on home till morning
All the men I have ever known were built from the ground up
With bricks solely made from tragedy
That have and always will
Provide a shaking foundation
With a raging ocean underneath
And few ways to get them home by morning

Never Ever Land

If you would be so gracious
Teach me to sew
I wish to return
Fabrics
Of long days
That speak of hard work
Or family traditions
Back to their former glory

Rectify

You're interesting
So captivating we could talk for hours
But you're just not one of the good guys
I know you'll break me
I know you won't live up to my expectations
I know that you'll make me realize why storms are named after people
It won't be your fault
I'm just a little older than this body
A little wiser than the years that this body is made of and maybe even
yours
But I will find a way to blame you
I wanted to care about you
And that's my problem
I want to care about everybody
You simply aren't ready
You don't know your own worth
It would be hard for you to show me mine
But I've learned you like constellations
the stars have always been a roadmap to me

Captivate

My dreams sit me down
To tell me stories of my deepest fears
They tell me of all they have seen
And discuss these scenes
That my subconscious sat on their doorstep
They tell me this load is heavy
But because of everything they have seen
They having a willingness to carry this
Only under the condition that
I keep dreaming big
Because the good things are so much greater
And they believe in them too

Responsibilities

Knowing your heroes in real life
Is both a gift and a weight
That is unexplainable in layman's terms

Expectations

And so the story goes
Magic must come from somewhere
Within
Or without
In my case
My magic came from both
Within the confines of the things that make me up
Without
Because the core of my woven wand
Is the thin lines of my grandmother's prayers
Her scripture etched into the inside
The outside
Leaves made of precious metals
Plucked from her heart of gold
So I only have magic of sympathy
Of good and empathy
Of trust and brighter days
Of arguments that can only be laid to rest
Of serenity not even the devil could test
Thin and long
Easy to wield and never heavy on the heart
Late night whispers of hope led my wand to me
Recognizing that I was the one
The one that my grandmother had been praying for
Waiting for
And lucky I was
That this
A goddess of a woman
Bided her time sending whispers to the wind
For me
Of which my wand will never let me forget
Every spell casted
A daily reminder
And some days the magic is wonky
Spells don't turn out as they should
An aguamenti may set the house on fire
As a gentle nudge

A mnemonic
A way of saying that there is still work to do
That I've not reached the serene heart
She prayed for me
And that maybe
I never will

Source

Girl you been stressed out
Running around. Going crazy
Tearing all the clothes out of the closet
Stop it
I promise to sit you down
Give you some room to let those papier-mâché lungs inflate

Too Close

I'd believe that this life consisted of more than forgotten notes and broken dreams
Sorrowful nights and moments stitched at their seams
Though there are people that would have you think otherwise
Because this life can get confusing
And it is never what it seems
I wish for you to know the beauty of the person staring back at you
And appreciate them
Because coffins don't come with room for more than one
And regrets never rest on two people's shoulders
After a while
I'm afraid you won't be afraid of destroying yourself anymore
I'm scared you might just wait on it
Like a package you expected in the mail
Pray that you know you're more than nasty words people said about you
Somewhere in your head know that
you don't have to be a diamond in the rough to be special
Life can be rough but that doesn't mean you're not special
Someone is ending their nights with prayers for you
Seems like people are always looking at everything through broken mirrors
All these distorted images changing reality
If you have disfigured views can that really be reality
I hope that mirror doesn't define you
Maybe one day you'll be brave enough to find you
Go find you
Journey far
Make a quest of finding home
For all that you have earned
The real you
The you that isn't catastrophe
Nor broken pieces of a mirror
The you that knows the difference between what it is and what it seems
The you with two feet firmly planted on the ground
Pure truth is crystalline
What it seems always lies in lands of dreams

Lands of make believe
And things unseen

What it seems

It is fine to realize you deserve better
Just because this world serves you scraps
Does not mean you are only meant to starve
Realize full belly and heart
It isn't required of you to be a leg of a table
That you will never eat at

Fed

In a newly defined fate
for myself I have
rewritten every line

I have had to stop and notice what it is to be alive
Felt this heart still beating
Still living against my rib cage
Chilled nights
Awaken goosebumps on my skin
And this night it is good to feel shivers run through my body
To be able to feel at all
What miraculous vigor
This warm blood still pumping through me
Life has not won the best of me yet

Alive and Well

For years I stayed
Silent
Hushed by the world and my parents and expectations
I was so scared of everything I wasn't
It was so funny when my mom told me she understood
Because every single time I would say to myself
No she doesn't
Everything a conjecture
Some people will tell you I was born to write
But I didn't put pen to paper until I was in the eighth grade
That was only two years ago
But it seems like lifetimes away from right now
the first time I ever heard slam poetry
This thing of significance
Caught my attention in a way nothing else had
The things they were saying
The way they expressed themselves
It was beautiful
It was the moment I fell in love with poetry
I wrote escape the first time worlds bleed from my mind to the pen and
onto paper
A 13 year old little girl who felt trapped in something she didn't
understand
Writing made me feel so alive
Made me feel like I had something to say
Almost like my words mattered
Like my little world that consisted of four walls mattered
Words have so much power
My best friend told me it was such an amazing poem
He'll tell you the same thing to this day
A year later you couldn't drag me away from the paper
I'd written more poems than I could count
I found Zora Howard and Alysia Harris on youtube
They again lit the same fire in my chest
Inspired me in so many ways
Alysia who refused to be that girl
In her Guiness skin

Zora with her won't die things
And her biracial hair
They just took me there
To a place where I would offer up my insides to the forest fire
If only to feel something
Poetry made me feel everything
No longer silent
But quietly in solidarity
No longer young dumb girl
I learned how deep I could get
How much I could understand with poems meant to be spoken word
With my poetry I learned how to define me
Finally found something to inspire me

Inspiration

Somewhere there's a house burning
Fire and smoke
Laying waste to wood and foundation
And here
Not far in the distance
Ash sprinkles down in the air
Like snow
Like new beginnings of cold weather
Billowing clouds of grey fill the atmosphere
Ghosts of could have been and would have been
If you listen quietly
You can hear the ghosts crackle against the wind
The way rushes of air
Only fan the flames
Tonight is the only time they wish for rain
Somewhere in the distance my house is burning
Soon to be a wastelands of used to be dreams
All those should have been things
How melting plaster
Gives way to creaky foundation
The house that might have been home
what a sincere interaction
Off there in the distance my house is burning
Some walls made of deceit
foundation almost questionable
And long before it's disappearance
I knew who lit the match

Where did the Flames Come From

Here I am again
My knees on the floor
My hands bound together
With a message against my lips
Something heavy on my heart
It all seems so hazy now
Isn't kneeling a form of surrender anyway
But here
Here in this space this yield has never felt more blissful
We often look at surrender like being shackled
No one wants to be vulerable
We've found ourselves forged from fire
Sons and daughters of strength
Not simply born but burned bright white hot into existence
Hell hath no wrath like the demands of strength in men
Heads held so high that low feels way too low
Heads held so high that pride almost seems snide in a way
So often our amour propre gets in the way
We've found ourselves abhorring any sign of downfall
Our lives revolve around relentlessness
We've forgotten how to give our problems up
We've forgotten that we don't have to carry the weight on our own
We have all come to deserve serenity
And for not being brave all the time there is not apology
Don't apologize for needing to be weak
This life can't be the end all be all
So don't tell us
Don't try to tell us that there is nothing that comes after this
Don't tell us that there is nothing to look forward to
Because we got so much more life left to face
And so much more hoping left to do
Don't tell us that we don't have any growth left in us
Because I haven't been kneeling here for no reason
And I'm just coming to learn that serenity is a necessity
Please
I need something to believe in
And kneeling has always been a friend of mine

My form of surrender just as it's always been
Being weak doesn't have to be a fault
Allow the waves of comfort to cradle you
We've all come to deserve peace
Being exhausted to the brink of breaking is not a prize to be won
It is a burn to be soothed
A wound to be salved
There will be pain but time goes on
And that's just life
Not weakness
We have all been left to the solace of our own minds at one point
Remember
It's not the scars you earn in battle that make you a warrior
It's the cause you were fighting for
And your ability to kneel here
Even after there seems like there's nothing left to fight for

Kneel

The world fell to dust
She went home
Where her stories were not her own
She told of all she'd seen out in our world
Of loud silences
That requires quiet mourning
She'd seen her fathers slaughtered
Her mothers raped
Her sisters taken
Her brothers worked to death
She saw the faces of those around her blow away like sand in the wind
Where were all her beautiful people going
She realized something
For the first time she said it aloud
They take all our people's umbrellas
Then spray bullets like thunderstorm
And ask us why we're angry that we got rained out
They make us obscure in their history books
Forgetting that we built everything in their history books
And everything constructed after that was laid on top our bones
They say don't be thugs
Keep yourself out of trouble
Get an education
Then the police won't mess with you
Let me see if I understand you
Philando Castile worked with kids everyday
Can you really say he was a thug
When do we end this massacre
Nobody wants to take the blame
America is so fortunate that the Black Lives Matter movement only
wants equality
And not revenge
America never used peace to gain its freedoms
How lucky they are now that we are trying to use peace to earn our's
Why is it that we have to dedicate so many hours
But we all know those 40 acres aren't coming
This system was built on our oppression

I can't help but feel like they never gave us umbrellas in the first place
We had to find our own
But by that time
They expected us to have accepted the rain

Umbrella

You been loving everybody but yourself
For way too long
Your petals are dying
It's okay to take a walk in the sun
Giving yourself water isn't hurting anyone else
Care for yourself
I swear it'll be worth it

No Sun Flower

And we would swear on the blood of every 20 something
That could still walk to their mom's house from home
that we would get out of here
Like 18 was our first class ticket out of here
But more like 18 is our very first ticket on a greyhound
to anywhere but home
Because 18 money ain't nothing like airplane fare
Cause we just know we're going to go so far away
Like nobody else that's lived in the same place their whole lives
had our same mind set
You know to every decade and a half nothing matters
BU
Before Us
We've become so comfortable in our surroundings
We are so quick to call our birthplace boring
The tribe of those who have raised us
becomes less and less appealing
We need escape
Need departure
Crave it like water
We have been thirsting so long for difference
Ready to rewrite the setting of our stories
Recast all the main characters
To start a new
To grow up
To regrow new roots
Even if that means uprooting our original tree
And facetiming mom
Rather than just knocking on her door
18 is so outlandish compared to all we have ever known
The freedom of the wind in our hair
Without the time constraint of the street lights
But only if we get out of here
The cobblestones of our old roads
Don't hold the same appeal anymore
A ticket for a greyhound feels like release
Feels like flowers in the spring

After the frost blows over
With none of the comfort of our mothers' doorsteps

Greyhound

Pan in on the garage
Only just arrived from work
My aunts sit with my mom
Speaking
Almost melodic conversation
I add when I feel apt to
Stay silent more than not
And
I bounce my leg
A habit I have grown to respect
Grown to accept
My aunt cuts conversation
Only to ask why I do it
"Your Titi do the same thing"
"I put my hand on her leg to get her to stop"
"You know that's a nervous condition right?"
Right..
"Well I have anxiety"
My mom's hands rush to me
Rub my back
Up and down
Friction of warmth and concern
"Mom, I don't have anxiety presently"
I only meant the disorder
But
She keeps her hands in motion
Devoted to the movement
"I know, I just love you"
And perhaps I needed that
My body knew I needed that
My shoulders relaxed
My lungs exhaled a breath I didn't know I was holding
A public show of my disorder
Something I don't do around family
I realize in later moments that
Maybe she was proud of me
Of my sharing so openly

It took years to find peace with me

Nervous Habit

He would sit
For hours
And he would explain things to himself out loud
It was like a recount of all the things that just transpired
I personally believe he was always trying to correctly prove himself
right in his mind
You see he is a complicated thing
When you talk ain't much going in
And there is a lot to figure out
I've come to the conclusion that he yells the way he does because he's
from havoc
Part fight and no flight
All take and no give
You'd have to come and see the way he tries to live
No power shall be formed against him
He can't take constructive criticism
He doesn't even understand that he is under construction
When you look at him
I mean really look deep into those abysses eyes
You can almost hear the tick tick tick
He's nonstop
He keeps going and going and going
I've tried to put blockades in his roadways
But that doesn't seem stop him
I try not to blame him
I remind myself where he comes from
I don't know where he's going
But he's paving the road himself
Jagged pathway
All hard day
All hardships
I try to remind myself of the way he lives
The things he saw
 All the catastrophe that his mind must be
And I think to myself
As I look at him I wonder if he can hear the tick tick tick
He's all chaos

And I can see that
It's just hard to grasp that
You see the good days are really good days
And the bad days are like David never slayed Goliath
Like Noah never built that arch
Like God never said let there be light
He tries
I have to know he does
Because that's where all my faith in him lies
It's hard to differentiate between his truth and his lies
He got all this discord but all the God in him
I can see it
But I don't know if he can see it
Dear god
THIS TICK TICK TICK
He has to hear it
It must be the cogs in his mind moving
Or maybe the men in his head working hard to keep the pieces wound
up
Or the civilization that makes up all the pieces of him living
Or all those nonstop thoughts moving at the speed of light and crashing
into each other at breakneck speeds
I'm waiting for the quiet
Right after the storm
When all is silent
I listen closely
Right now it's just him and all his thoughts
It's peaceful
There's not anger or hurt
All the havoc has settled
The discord has deceased
The catastrophe has quit
And I wonder if he can hear his own tick tick tick

Tick

Here comes all this heat
And me
A sapphire of gems
Made from the cooling of rock
How am I to survive
This heat wave of losing friends
When all I have ever known
Was my own cold

Surviving my Emotions

Somewhere along the lines
My hurt grew me tender
Grew me kind and softer than before
Wanting nothing more than
To be the opposite of what hurt me
Cracks grew in this concrete
And vines and flowers began to
Seep through
This is me healing
This is becoming all my past could never be
How good it is to be broken
To create something new
Of what you used to be
Life has risen from what was thought
to be an unbreakable foundation
There is pride in this
I am learning to live again

To Siaara who taught me this lesson

Reverence

Mourning brings many things in its suitcases
It comes with all this baggage that will take days to unpack
And it seems like it'll take even longer to pack all these things back up
and send mourning on its way
There are a lot of things you didn't want to deal with
Didn't want to feel
These days that pain isn't welcome in my home or my heart
For I refuse to cry over life lost when there was no life lost at all
No life doesn't come and go like rainfall
Life is forever here and is to be celebrated
It demands to be celebrated
I have lost no memory of those passed on
I can still feel them in my heart
Their spirits fistful in each breath that I take
Though it be sad to see them go I can never forget all the things they
taught me
Never forget what an amazing life they lived
And all the things they left behind
Yes they won't be here now
But someday I'll see them again
Someday
Their memory stays as daytime as it's always been
So bright and full of life
No definition of their true light
I hate to see them go
But what a beautiful life they lived
All the amazing things they had to give
Days past
And time may not last
But it does heal all wounds
And things are going to be okay soon
Maybe not today
But sometime in the future it won't be like this anymore
I don't know when
But the pain will pass
And time may not last but it does heal all wounds

Morning will come
And with it a brighter tomorrow

Mourning

There is something so peaceful about the darkness of my room
At half past five
When the sun starts peeking out of the clouds
The only thing to break the silence is the constant hum of my fan
The outside world has yet to wake
A few headlights dance pass my windows
In the early morning wake of the world
Everything feels so new
The sins of the night passed
Fresh morning dew
You can feel the potential of the day before you
You can still see the moon slipping away
You can feel how the stars yearn for the sun
But the night creeps out silently
Careful not to wake the resting
If you listen close enough you can hear the spark of the world ignite
At something like a quarter past six
Mothers are waking their children
Fathers already packed up and off to work
All this cool day sunlight
And all this riotous feet against pavement
It's kind of hard to make it
To keep up
Don't miss the bus
Make the train
And somehow here I am still laying in bed
Oblivious to all this fast paced non stop moving around me
Shades closed
The sun hitting my floor like the forgotten laundry from the night
before
And the world around me is awake and moving
That young boy on the street with five dollars in his pocket
And a day of a whole lot of nothing to keep up with
There's something in his smile
Like sunshine
Like I don't know where you came from or where you're going
That glint in his eyes brighter than the spark of the world

All while I can lay in complete silence
The hum of my fan as my only company
There's a big fast paced world around me
And here I am
Laying in a bed where vivid dreams have been long forgotten
Where nothing outside these four dull walls matters
Cast away hide away
In my very own world amongst worlds
And in the aftermath of my sleep I'll plan forever's in spaces where
most only see temporary

Half Past Morning

Entreat you to know me
I have left behind so much
To be the sort of weightless that you need
Perceive all the music I had to
Turn away from
Because you have often preferred silence
Cut the notes away from my skin
As apologies
For my singing that is not to your liking

Lost Melodies

They are present

                    unseen

There in one specific moment

                    And gone

the next
A whisper of the wind
on an otherwise perfect day

                    I almost feel crazy

Until they reassure me
That I am indeed

                    Being followed

The source of their peace

                    A beacon of hope for the weary

An ode to those who didn't find their intent

                    In this life or the next

They attach themselves to me

                    Ever deserving of serenity

Chills across my arms

                    I know they are here

But I can't find it in me to ask them to go

                    Afterall

What Goddess am I

                    To banish the sick and tired from
                      all they knew

In their hereafter

Following

My whole life I've learned to be all quiet
I fold myself in silence
Am I outgoing
Yes
Opinionated and loud
Of course
But I learn to keep peace
Like the time keeper
I make sure everything happens when it should

Aftermath

It is my belief that we meet as many mothers as we need
In this life of challenge
And tribulation
I have found mother is the synonym for so many words
Mother be healer
Be guide
Be faith
Be constant reminder
Be teacher
Be helper
And shelter
Be love
And unconditionally
Be breath when need be
In truth mother's form into anything we need them to be
Mothers recognize any necessity and pour their heart into that glass
I have met so many mothers
In teachers
Coworkers
Friends
And somehow they are all essence of the matter of mind
In the same way my mother is
They are functioning in unimaginable ways
While still not even reaching full capacity
Uncountable generations of women
Always needed
Having raised nations
Carried them on their backs and shoulders
While still standing in impeccable posture
They create life in any circumstance
And ask for nothing in return
They chase death out of the doors with sole glances
With comfort and softness

Needed

To dissipate
To have everything and turn it into nothing
Could we only define this as fool
Only see this as wasteful
Make this only empty sky
With not a cloud in sight
Despite the craving of rain
This sun can be unforgiving
Dry and beating down
How do we survive this dissipation
Of everything that
Needs our own water to survive

Rainless

And it's so hard sometimes
To want to get up with all those shadows holding you down
When everything seems kind of pointless
When the only thing you do out there is apologize
So many people say you're lazy
Say you're making excuses
But they don't truly understand
the hollows and abysses that have
Made their home inside of you
They don't understand that "doing something that makes you happy"
doesn't make you happy
Depression cannot be wished away with positive words
Sometimes you just don't care anymore
And it's not your fault
And you can't stop it
But they can't grasp that
And you can't mask that
You can't hide away from it
And you can't help but remember when you weren't afraid of the things
inside of you
Now you're demons live closer than your neighbors do
And at this point you don't know what to do
There has been this steady erosion
It comes in random spurts that leave you feeling less and less yourself
Hardly the monument you used to be
Sometimes this is all the time
All your hope seems to be shatter
And here you are still trying
People tell you that you have no reason to be sad
But you can't help it
And they aren't really helping
Telling you it's just phase
Telling you that it'll pass
But they have no idea how long this could really last
And you've had your head under water for way too long
You just don't have that much air
Get to feeling like what's the point anyway

It's all pointless either way
I remember a time when there was no effort involved
When happiness came natural
But you keep trying
Even though times are trying
And we live here
In the hollows of the abysses that used to stay here
Not dying but survived by strength unmeasurable to those who haven't
experienced it
And I'm proud of you
Because you keep trying
Even though times are trying

This too Shall Pass

If it brings you any joy
Or sense of sustenance
To be alluring uncharted land
Be that
This mystery of wild and untouched
In every sense
Don't allow anyone
To take this joy of magnitudes unbeknownst to the world
Live vivaciously
Love in vitality
Dance with sunsets
And kiss sunrises in the same
wake
Know it well
You have deserved and earned any piece of happiness
You desire

New Territory

I always know the time
As I know where the sun resides
As the moon takes solace hanging in the sky
Each and every burning ball of gas
A tick on my watch
Both hands made of shooting stars

Time Telling

To guardians of heart and happiness
There is magic
In meeting girls
With lit hearths for eyes
The way they can open their chests
And show you home
Beyond all you have known
Small sparks of smiles
Create a fire that can warm you
Inside out
These blessings of girls
That deserve the same warmth they give out
They make the night sky feel small
And less lonely
Like it's something they hold in their pocket
And break pieces off of
Just to give to you when you need to feel
At home again
There are spells in their embraces
Easy for them to hex your problems away
Laughing with them for hours
Can feel like meditation
Perform like forgetting
Weights of worlds
So instant connection
Easy breathing
And flowers in your lungs
A tenderness that brings you back from the brink
There is magic in this
These true connections
Sacredness in their sensitivities
A knowingness in their sensibilities
They give you everything you need
Are drink and food of the soul and celestial
They know that we rise to the amount of love we are given
Just as we do expectations and dire situations
They are abundance

They are midnight calls to the hopeless
And bringing life back into focus
This world is ever undeserving of such limitless love
These girls are deserving of all the magic they are
And all the love they have to give

Friends

Meals have always been a time of blessings and laughter
This contentment should be cherished
After All the food was hot
The laughs were loud
And mama spent too much time cooking
For us not to enjoy ourselves

Memories

Bundled up in a coat
Cold nose
Gloves and boots
These are small comforts that you know
Against the cold
Somehow
Against all odds
The chill still weasels its way in
It is always trying to get close and wrap around you
You can feel it seeping through the windows
Even as you go inside
It stays wrapped around your toes
The cold is wanting
You
This allure of heat
Everything it could never be
This isn't violence
But soft caress
The cool clings to your clothes
Even after you leave it
And welcomes you fully
As soon as you return
No anger for having left in the first place
No despair for your constant need of escape
How is it that love
Is most unconditional
From those we shun
Over and over

Undeserving

What a forest life is
And here you are
Tied yourself down to a dying tree
The trunk is rotten
All the leaves have lost their green
And you
Keep watering this shriveled plant
As if your tears will bring it back to life
Willing to die with it
unwilling to live without it
You cannot eat
Do not sleep
And yet here
This tree you dedicated your life to
Remains un-growing
Still rotting
Can't you smell it's flesh
You have not born it a new life
What soft heart does this bring you
No ease of the mind
To watch a tree that was never yours die

Oak

We are all dying
And everyday we chose to live anyway
Is this a resistance
Long live the regime
May we know
Days
And months
And years
Beyond all odds
We have not ended yet

Life

Somehow grief makes us better
Sadness and fear can make us bigger
Make us better people
Help us to love our loved ones more
Be more gracious
And grateful
Hold them closer
Never wanting to let go
They make us cherish
Regain lost focus
Press more kisses to the backs of their hands
Whisper to them often
Makes us bigger people
More able to accept apologies we may never receive
Forgive
Maybe forget some too
Be loving
And offer grace to those who once wronged us
We are creatures
Who learn
By being scared of the possibility
Of no more

We Learn From Loss

There exists space where I am infallible
Where fault and fear do exist
But offer no hindrance
Or higher ground
Water
With no risk of drowning
There is a vastness of beautiful oceans
And no danger to it
Diving in
But my lungs no longer felt the heaviness
Of depth
Somehow air goes unneeded
With no words left unsaid
This is childhood
This is blissful ignorance and maybe even
Arrogance
But let it be that
For the sands of time have yet to move here
And the ease of hours
Still pours down slow like molasses
Sweet
Unphased by days
Somewhere this is the treasure of legends
And somehow I have captured it
On my concrete front porch
The sunset falling behind horizon
lit my ocean up
Like christmas lights
And this is touching God
This is true youth unspent
Innocence is such a concept to have captured
In a moment such as this I hold an hourglass in my hands
The grains have not yet moved
Since my grasp has touched it
I am truly untouchable
When I take no leave and no loss
The vast ocean is made from the water

Of the fountain of youth

Young

Playing make believe feels so familiar
Still to this day
I would play black smith
To build the smiles that mean the most to me
Risk burns
And fatigue
Make them strong
Unbreakable teeth
Forged from unimaginable heat
Somehow as children we easily formed into everything we could be

Cast Iron

I have learned to call my body gospel
I have learned to call my body temple
I have learned to know my body is sanctuary
I have learned
I have learned
I have learned
I have learned that because your body regenerates so many cells every
7 years you are basically brand new
But I still carry these scars
I will always carry these memories
I have learned not to take revenge on my body
I am learning to forgive myself
I have found a way to forgive those I have resented because they didn't
see it
I am getting better
And everyday is recovery
Everyday is a new beginning
I had to stick around to know it got better
I wish I could tell a younger me that it does get better
I have bared my soul to a hollowed sky
With no return from the stars for my trouble
And learned to be a peace with that
I had to learn to be at peace with myself
I learned my worth
Those nights coaching myself to breathe again will never feel like a
distant memory
Some days I just didn't want to get up
But something in me never let me give up
I questioned if this was all worth it
I wondered if I was really worthy
Maybe I was more burden than loved one
But I am here
I am here not in spite of my experiences but because of them
Sometimes being broke down makes room for bigger improvements
I learned that especially on the worst days I am the daughter of a king
who always goes before me
And I continue to learn

Because everyday is a new journey
This is why I only saw my family a couple times a week
This is why we all lived in the same household but we're worlds apart
This is why when people called I ain't answer
Pick up the phone just to toss it to the side
This right here is why I used to let everything slide
This is why you'll hear me say "you don't know me, not really. Not the way you think you do."
This is why my character came into question
This is why people wouldn't hear from me anymore
This is why I have to learn
Because without growth the only path would be destruction
Because without hope the only path would be devastating
There are days when I forget that every grain that has been made of me is brilliant skyline
Days when I forget that I am stardust and comets
Days when I forget that I'm just plain worth it
And I know God
And I know everyone else has these days too
We all have to learn too
There are just days when you don't want to get out of bed
I understand that too
And so
I stand here before you
Laying my soul at the feet of a hollowed sky
Because I have to learn too

Hollowed Sky

Each of us press from
Hurting to healing
Still know the natural disaster of the missing parts
That make us whole
Oh holy
Others have come in and marked this land
Sacrificial
Built their houses of worship in a place
That did not belong to them
Praising of these false Gods
Who do not know of true value and worth
They can see this boldly painted sky
Of blood
And plum
And only see a sky
They won't last through hurricane season
Never bothered to ask the people who were here before them
What the climate is like
They don't know how you have already become accustomed
To the way harsh rains cling to your skin
You have been bathed in flood waters your whole life
This baptism of falling water
And know this to be healing
While they can only drown
They have angered the divine of this land
Trying to inhibit this process of patching up
They will learn why hurricanes are named after people
The wrath of hurt can be so consuming
That one may become a trinity of wind and rain and flood
If only to sit at the eye of the storm
To offer calm to themselves
Even if that means destroying the landscape around them
Especially if that means
Destroying these invaders around them
To reclaim all that was theirs in the first place
I know your pain
Respect your rage

I myself have turned into a natural disaster when need be
And learned to worship my own will after
This reclamation of being
They did not know we would take ourselves back

Hurricane Season

My heart has beat a tattoo into my ribcage
The imprint is comfortable
How thankful I am now
That my heart feels at home inside my chest
Prayed for
The lessening of the consistent ache
I'm okay with this hearth that my heart
Has made of my lungs

Comfort

I have fallen in love with birth charts
With the ways the stars align on each person's day and time
We hese small beings of light and matter
Being dictated by these large astral bodies
It fascinates me
Bewitched by the magic of it all
The push and pull of
The way planets make playground
Of who we are
Let me read you
I want to know how the stars have
Left their pitter patter foot prints
In the sand that is you
How each shift in the galaxy is another tide
Washing the old away
Do you know what retrograde is
Would you think me crazy
If I asked where and when you were born
To find out who you are
And who you are meant to be

What's Your Rising

How have you decorated your home
Once you moved out into this world
On your own
Does each piece have meaning
Have you honored your mother and father's hard work
And worn hands
Do you cook meals
And clean the counters before bed
Or have you chosen to forget all you have ever known

Traditions

I don't think anyone pays attention to the small things while falling
Most of the time they let the terror consume them
Don't ever stop to see the beautiful things
Don't ever look to see the star lit sky almost hugging them
Can't feel the wind around them cradling them
Holding them close
As if to say I don't want to let you go

Moments

My mother holds my breath in her heart shaped locket
Feels it in her own chest when mine is tightening
Began to know my woes well
I have always been this part of her
But long since my birth this place in her
Has been quiet
Suddenly she can feel this staggering heartbeat in her locket
Heart shaped burns against her chest
The little scars become apart of her
A part of me
She calms me
Her voice calming the flame
That floats me like an air balloon
13 years old felt more like plummeting than flying
Not to mention that altitude sickness from getting up everyday
She calms the flame
Years later
Some days more flying missile
Than simple air balloon
She can still feel my breath fanning the flames
In her heart shaped locket

Float

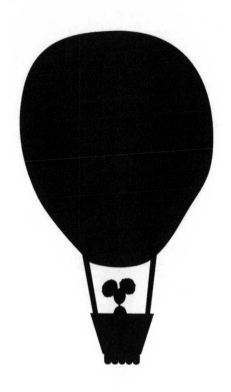

Your name was the last to pass my lips
You saw right through me
I could feel the vibrations of your soul
Almost like it remembered me
All I could experience in that moment was your amazing energy
Because of you I find nourishment in the oddest of places
Your hands
My gateway to easy breathing
Your embrace
The way it comforts me
Feeds me when I'm malnourished
The way the sun rays cradle me
Like a mother to her newborn babe
Laughter be a melody
Oh sweet lullaby
Your voice was always so musical
Summertime
Degrees sky high
and still you put chills through me
I could spend hours on end
Floating in this river
Existing in this water
Like the nile carrying me to the all knowing Sphinx
Miles away from here
So many life times away from here
Your voice will still soothe me
Even galaxies away where I'll find new age wisdoms from old munks
None of them would ever be your comfort
No one would venture to try and take your place
And winds seem to carry all my doubts away
Taking all these fears away
I become fearless all while finding nourishment in the oddest of places
And this feeling embodies a Goddess like presences
How I would worship this Goddess until the end of my days
Her smile breathtaking
Her laugh whimsical
Her name be peace

And still in all her glory she'll never dare to be your comfort
Her hands never my gateway to easy breathing
Never in lifetimes away from here will her voice soothe me the way
your's has always been able to
I don't know if its possible
But if it is I wish to live for you
Dedicate lifetimes to all the things you taught me
Oh how it would be beautiful
Almost as beautiful as the marvel that is your mind
I've felt the touch of your silken skin and been at peace
Saw the way your chest rises and falls with each breath
Like night times sweep away sunlight
And I have truly known peace

Peace

Please follow
These lights that guide you home
They have run directly through you
Been in contact with your core
These lights make up smiles
And moments that can only be remembered in them
It breathes
This is seeing the lights in your house
After a cold walk home
Knowing that you will see warmth soon
It is the kiss of a lover
After extended time away
Absorb it
This light
Makes miles
Feel like minutes

Soul

My God has told me to be still
There were no mistakes made
This story is still being written
There is still work left to be done

J Belong to

Dear women of the nations
I wish I could reach you better
Stretch across this language barrier to a place of understanding
I will in due time
But until then
Don't be apologetic for your language
The way your home dances from your vocal cords is beautiful
Keep your stubborn tongue
Never allow this imperialist culture
To shove this bulk of unkindly speak down your throat
Stay as home as you can be
For as long as you can be
Let your mother's words
Cradle you
And put you to sleep at night
Remain your daughter's
Cool pool of all your home ever was to her
These snakes men
Of foreign lands
Will try to steal
All of the history from your teeth
Try to boa constrictor all your ancestry from your throat
And this world may let them
But I know that you will never let them
You
Goddesses of women
With the world on your back and
The next generation on your shoulders
The last resting inside the column of your throat
And all this home still growing in your belly
Family draped over you
I pray you proud of your beautiful language
Of those that came before you
And those you will teach
After you
A lineage worth more than these invisible lines
That men put in the dirt

Barriers only seem to be something built by men
To keep us out
To keep something in
And then here you are
All brazen works
Your feet and hands
Artifacts
New roots and branches of old family trees
Proud
And I know one day
I will reach you
Where leaves meet sky

Language Barrier

I always believed in the power of water
The way it heals
And holds
Speak things on and into it
Pulling yourself under the water and staying there
Just holding your breathe
Solstice of problems melting away
Let it all go down the drain
Call this brujeria
Magic
Or Manifest
Water has always been the cure-all
Passed from mothers to daughters
Know it well
Clear blue of limitless possibilities
Deep sea dive into infinite realities
She cradles you
Sings you to sleep
And dulls the noise
This water that you came from
Birthed and raised
A beginning and end
There is pride in this heritage
She has hoped to make an aesthete of you

Names Water takes On

We exist
In the sweet breaths of a Goddess
That allows storms
Only when she feels necessary
This lazy topple of all the things
She has left unsaid
All the things we mean to be before becoming who we are
Where nothing truly matters

Hold

Have we not all been new beginnings
Truths for someone who has only ever known lies
Greetings for those that experienced
The most painful of goodbyes
From time to time
We take the form of the things
That people around us need
If only to pacify them
Us
To grow trust
And show love
And perhaps these aren't easy feats
Not saving people from fates
But a comfort that we may never understand
We
The tender of heart
And softest of hands
Become what those around us need
Not to save lives
But to make days
Easier
We are what cushions the fall
The safety blanket and whispers that blow darkness away

Alleviate

They told me about this
How one day we would all meet our match
And that day
The events of that day would leave you tongue tied and light headed
Your stomach a cage for fluttering butterflies
Your heart no more than a stone skipping across a lake
They say it would be a date not to be forgotten
Each planet and star would align
It would be perfect
The first time poetry ever spoke to me was 5th grade
In a dark classroom
Of a community school
A man told me of how he couldn't read
And there I was
In awe of how he laid his heart break on the stage
In love with
What I didn't know
Would be the love of my life
My child's bedtime stories will be poetry
They will know the eloquence of words
Before their ABCs
Will know sonnets better than lullabies
They will be the only thing I love more than spoken word
Poetry saved me
Gave me a place to call home
In years when I was so lost I couldn't even find myself
So call it a damn savior complex
But know
Here I bleed my stories like ink to paper
I lay my spirit at your feet
And feel at home within myself
Finally able to believe the walls of this body
Won't crumble in on me
Finally at peace enough to sleep
Tuck myself in and listen to this staggering heart beat
This is living
This is finding what you love enough

To realize how much you value yourself
This heart beat a sweet melody
Forever lullaby

Bedtime Stories

Sweet Dreams

I have found
treasure in myself.
Named it joy
and been glad in
it. We are those
most deserving of
love. Pray we
find it in those
who deserve it too.

Yours Truly,

Nashé

What happens
When the glitter fades
And suddenly I don't sparkle like you're used to
Will you hold me with reluctance
Will your pride diminish
No longer the trophy you saw me as
Sometimes the shine of the night fades away
I'm left to wonder if you'll stay

Everything that Glitters

In my life I have never felt more alive than in times when nobody had
to tell me I was
I have made religion of moments that I don't have to remember to know
that I was happy in them
I've been open to the spectacle of the night
just to feel bathed in the stars
I have needed that

Moments

My neighborhood was under construction for a multitude of years
The air around the new houses always smelled sweeter
This is potential
Where house could finally meet home
Bless every set of hands
Working to build a place
That will one day
Be the focal point
Of a happiness that so many yearn for
If the universe is willing

Home

After Winston Duke and his Black man joy induced by the adoration of Black women

Your brown boy joy is important
And as I await the quickly approaching arrival of Dru Amari Brown Jr
I write you this
For my future son and my god son
As your mother I write you this
Dear baby boy
Be happy
If I teach you nothing else
I hope I teach you that I value your joy over all
You deserve
Laughter of sunrises
And days that make it so you never want the sun to set
You are important
And adored
Jewels and melanin of dripping gold
Shining brighter than diamonds or rubies
Be radiant
Beautiful little brown boy
That I have loved since far before your conception
I love you vastly
Indefinitely
Deeper than the depths of oceans
Seas of impossible potential all in your belly
I love you astronomically
Far beyond the extent of galaxies
Stars crushed into every single one of your teeth
Automatically
Because it just feels so natural
Only for you
Of infinite strength and grace
You make it easy so to grow pride like you have the greenest thumb
This side of the milky way
How the masses should sing your name like hymns
Be ecstatic

Though the world may not know it yet
It is yours
The world belongs to you

Things I Must Teach my Son, Addendum

It's okay that you are still learning to forgive this body
To stop demanding reparations of the lonely
Surviving is the biggest favor you ever did yourself

Love for This Body

I have existed in nothing
Tossed a life to the sea
Brazenly losing it all
With no bravery behind it
Oblivion
I have learned that I can be absolutely absence
Out of sight
Smoke in the air
Here one moment and gone the next
Nothing
I also found I can be everything
Be all the love within me
All the God inside me
Leading my way into myself
A caravan of both loss and gain
Everything returns to dust
What comforting emptiness
Sweet Oblivion
Being so okay with the trip back to center
Loss only a side effect of returning
To all I have ever known
The light inside
It can not die
My world has ended so many times
Made dust of me
But it has returned
Many times as I
Have slept at night

Oblivion

My pain has been made into language
Painted onto stages
Brought onto the world show
And here is where I find my peace
Not just to speak my truth
But to
Understand it
To act on it and heal
Not only to accept my soul at the foot of a hollowed sky
With no response
But patch the wounds from
That bruise to
My happiness

Hollowed Sky Healing

An ode to my best friend
And this other worldly task you had to create something new
You have existed
While creating new existence
Birthed a whole new solar system
Created a smile that will last a lifetime
Every atom
A brand new star or planet
You created heavenly bodies
Made a God of you
To have known life
And born it into this world
You are so deserving of this fresh start
Of feeling a love that is all encompassing
Your body has stretched to fit whole constellations
Named them each
His toes
His hands
His breath
We thank God for every minute
Everything leading up to now
Every blue raspberry slushie
Every late night trip to a store for whatever ice cream
Was your taste that night
Holy offering
We
A tribe blessed with a new beginning
And you
Goddess of will
Maker of men
Bringer of new life
A sacrificial divine
And he
The novice
All he has ever known leading up to his birth
Is you
Starting with a hunger only a mother can sate

There is so much I want to know
Want to understand
What it means to live and be life
To be the builder of nations

The Divine

Just say you will
And so be it
You will
If things are on earth
As they are in our celestial here after
Then you will
Manifest all that your life should be
All that you want it to be
And it will
This existence will bend to your will
Your hand the mover a mountains
The universe will recognize your voice
And know to shift
As in truth you are the creator
Of all things that you push your life towards
Know that you are deserving of this magnificent
Existence
Pray this finds you well
Hope you know your own power
Before these lights go out

You Will

You're a page turner
A novel that is easy to never put down
A hard back worn from time
With several of your pages dogeared to keep a place
A story that should be reread over and over
I promise to value you
Treat your plot with importance
And put you on the shelf only to store you
I know I'll reach for you again before I even realize

Treasured Books

These words
The words that plague my mind every time a muse is in the midst
Something kind of like euphoria
As these words escape my lips
Something buried under these words
More than emotion
More than love or hate or sadness
I don't think I can make it clear to you
You would have to go on this journey with me
Be open to all these new feelings
It may not be clear
There are a lot of different energies
I can't help but love the vibe
In this spiritual place
This space that
Gave me peace of mind
A space to express myself
And something like a poetic soul
Something like
This river of healing flows through me
Right before the sky bends
Before this earth cracks and I fall through
I just want to thank you
For lending listening ears
This space only holds beauty to me
And these words like religion
These words always hold me faithful
Always bring me peace
This creative space like my Genesis
Something like a poetic soul
Like a craftsmen to his craft
Forever dedicated
Keeping me afloat
Know what it feels like to fall in love with the spirit of words
More than metaphors or similes
More like a life forces in these assemblies
Assemblies of words and vibes

Of people from all walks of life
These words like religion
These words that hold so many people faithful

Dialogue of the Faithful

Allow me to serve as your daily reminder
That every black and brown girl
Holds infinite value
Your poetry is important
Your paintings are important
Your art is important
Every breath of star dust that enters and leaves your lungs is important
I have not forgotten you
Not forsaken what is the gem garden of your insides
The rose quartz of your mind
And the amethyst that lines your belly
I cherish the emerald of your chest
And the ruby up and down your legs
You
This boundless source of healing
Unattainable fixers touch
It is no wonder they wish to take everything from us
If only to be what we are
You rising phoenix
Your diamond soul has never been shaken by the ash this world tries to
make of you
You are stronger than this world would have you be
Immense
Vast
Immeasurable
Untold treasure of ages
And I pray you stay this way

Gem Garden

A dwelling
Defined as a place one has lived in
Dwell
To think speak or write about at length
Grammie always said
You can't dwell on the things you can't change
Everyday as the sun comes up you are filled with joy
Ecstatic to have known light
And everyday as sunset nears
As it comes and goes
You weep
To the dark of the night sky
All you see is the empty of it all
Never the heavenly body of moon or stars
Only this void of day
This is to have seen your pain previously
Been held in its embraced and then willing returned
Despite the collapsing of your chest as a constant
In absence of a fire
Somehow you still find smoke here
I know this brash
See how there is no eutony of it
I pray you
A child of wisdom
Learn to know it too
Sunset is inevitable
And tears tell a story
So allow those of your past
To tell the story of no more
You have seen it
The sun sink in the sky everyday
To be replaced by the moon
Familiarize yourself with
The way it can whelve itself into the pit of you
And it has not moved
Your cries have never stopped the sun from setting
You cannot dwell on what you cannot change

Here I ask you
To know the moon as you have the sun
Accept Your sunset
For the moon always comes
And with it
Brings healing

Dwell

Thank you

CPSIA information can be obtained
at www.ICGtesting.com
Printed in the USA
BVHW071624110319
542310BV00017B/1604/P